A TRIP TO THE
POLICE STATION

Josie Keogh

PowerKiDS press™

New York

Published in 2013 by The Rosen Publishing Group, Inc.
29 East 21st Street, New York, NY 10010

First Edition

Editor: Amelie von Zumbusch
Book Design: Ashley Drago

Photo Credits: Cover © UpperCut Images/age fotostock; pp. 5, 17, 18, 22 Shutterstock.com; p. 6 Darrin Klimek/Digital Vision/Thinkstock; pp. 9, 10 Jupiterimages/Photos.com/Thinkstock; p. 13 Darrin Klimek/Digital Vision/Getty Images; p. 14 © www.iStockphoto.com/Darren Mower; p. 21 UpperCut Images/Getty Images; p. 24 (middle) iStockphoto/Thinkstock.

Library of Congress Cataloging-in-Publication Data

Keogh, Josie.
 A trip to the police station / by Josie Keogh. — 1st ed.
   p. cm. — (Powerkids readers: my community)
 Includes index.
 ISBN 978-1-4488-7405-7 (library binding) — ISBN 978-1-4488-7484-2 (pbk.) —
 ISBN 978-1-4488-7558-0 (6-pack)
 1. Police—Juvenile literature. I. Title.
 HV7922.K48 2013
 363.2—dc23
                                    2011051406

Manufactured in the United States of America

CPSIA Compliance Information: Batch #CS12PK: For Further Information contact Rosen Publishing, New York, New York at 1-800-237-9932

CONTENTS

The Police Station   4
A Police Dog   8
Officers   12
Words to Know   24
Index   24
Websites   24

We went to the police station.

6

Pat's dad is the chief.

We met a police dog.

His name was Max.

We saw Officer May's badge.

Joe tried on her hat.

We saw Officer Reed's car.

17

18

Then he had to go.

19

A man stole a car.

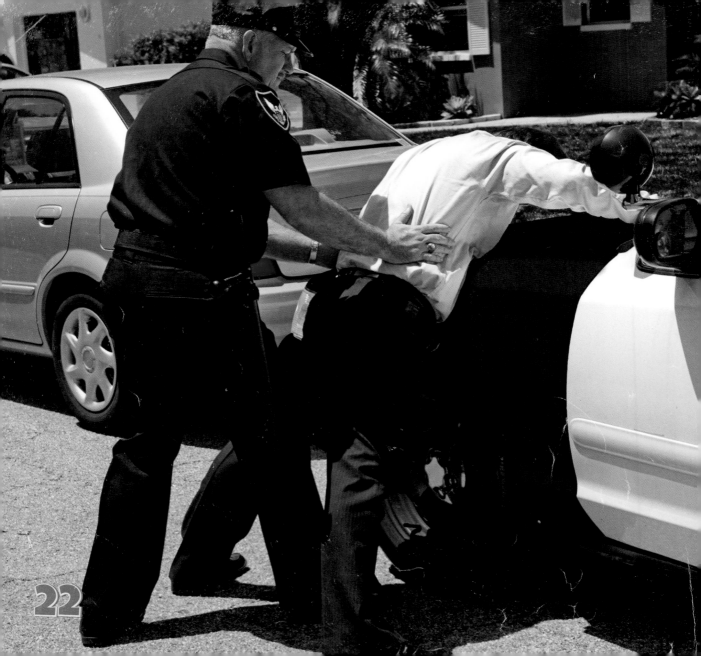

The police caught the man!

WORDS TO KNOW

arrest: To hold someone by law.

criminal: A person who breaks the law.

uniform: Clothes worn by a group of people.

INDEX

D
dog, 8

H
hat, 15

N
name, 11

P
police, 23

WEBSITES

Due to the changing nature of Internet links, PowerKids Press has developed an online list of websites related to the subject of this book. This site is updated regularly. Please use this link to access the list:
www.powerkidslinks.com/pkrc/police/